JOURNEY BEYOND

Books by Ivy Northage

Mediumship Made Simple
Spiritual Realisation

JOURNEY BEYOND

Trance talks by Chan,
spirit guide of

IVY NORTHAGE

LIGHT PUBLISHING

First published by The Spiritualist Association of Great Britain in May 1970 as
Trance Talks by "Chan", Guide of Ivy Northage

Published by Psychic Press 1972 as *Journey Into Spirit*
Reprinted 1974, 1981
Second Edition entitled *Journey Beyond* 1988
Reprinted 1993

This edition published in 1997 by
LIGHT PUBLISHING
at the College of Psychic Studies
16 Queensberry Place
London, SW7 2EB

ISBN: 0 903336 29 4

The aim of LIGHT PUBLISHING at The College of Psychic Studies is to explore all aspects of spiritual and psychic knowledge.
The views expressed in all books published by LIGHT PUBLISHING at the College of Psychic Studies are those of the author, and do not necessarily reflect the views of The College of Psychic Studies.

"We have room for all who realise the importance, in a materialistic age, of expressing a belief that there is something behind matter and that death does not end all..."
From a preliminary meeting of the College, November 1883. This was the declared note of the then new College and it remains so to this day.

Printed in Great Britain by Booksprint

CONTENTS

FOREWORD

JOURNEY BEYOND is a selection from the transcripts of three lectures given by CHAN in 1951. Society's needs were very different at that time, when almost everyone suffered bereavement as a result of the war. During the intervening years, CHAN'S long association with the requirements of people in all walks of life must have widened his experience and the essence of his communication. Birth and death remain the same, however, although the circumstances may vary.

In this book CHAN emphasises that each person is an individual and wholly responsible for their own actions. While the reality of survival after death must remain the foundation of conviction, once people have accepted this they want to know how the loved one is faring. What is happening to them? What sort of life are they leading? He reiterates that what he describes relates to his own experiences, and admits with his customary humility that there could be other levels of consciousness above and beyond his own. He substantiates this by quoting Spiritualism's seventh principle, "Eternal progress is open to every human soul". If we accept this as a reality, we must also accept that there are many different levels of progress.

What CHAN tells us has been his own personal experience, and includes the knowledge of his most recent incarnation, together with what he has acquired since he came into the full realisation of his spiritual identity. "I am," he says, "surrounded by many such spirits on the same level as myself, although our experiences may be quite different".

The essence of individuality is very important, because some of the things he tells us may conflict with what we have read or even what we have received from our own Spirit Guides. He examples this with cultures from another country that would be unacceptable to us, but right for them.

If you find yourself rejecting anything in the book do not allow this to confuse or distress you; it must not diminish your own convictions or beliefs while they bring you comfort. The closing statement of CHAN'S introduction is as follows,

"I SOLEMNLY SWEAR TO YOU AS A MESSENGER OF THE SPIRIT WORLD, UPON THE LEVEL TO WHICH I BELONG, THESE HAVE BEEN MY EXPERIENCES".

While I can take no personal credit for the subject matter in this book, it has been a great privilege to be used as an instrument for what I know has been a source of comfort and upliftment to so many people.

IVY NORTHAGE
April, 1997

PREFACE

I, as an emissary from the spirit world, can only speak to you
with the knowledge that I myself possess. I want you to understand that there are realms of consciousness and truth hitherto
untapped by myself, and many other spiritual guardians, and
emphasise that while I tell you what I know to be true in my own
experience, there could be other messengers whose experience is
wider and more profound than mine, who may to a certain extent
contradict what I tell you.

It is not really a contradiction, but it is a confusion that could
arise from limited knowledge. I fail to see how we can avoid
this, when one of our most important spiritual principles is
"Eternal progress open to every human soul".

Now, if we accept that eternal progress is open to every human
soul, we must have degrees and levels of progression which
must be relative to particular individuals and must limit their
knowledge in greater or lesser degree.

So, what I shall tell you has been my own personal experience.
It will include knowledge of my last and most recent reincarnation and also that which I have acquired since I came into the full
realisation of my own spiritual identity.

This is not so only in my own case, but in that of my contem-
poraries of similar spiritual development, for I am surrounded by
many beings like myself, who have had similar experiences to
myself. We are on a sort of common level, since all our experiences have been much the same, although they have been for

different reasons and in different directions.

It is important, dear friends, that you understand this, because some of the things that I shall say to you may conflict with what you have read or even what you have received from your own spirit guides. Don't let this deter or confuse you. Realise this is a very large universe. For instance, if you were to be told about certain customs and habits in another country, you might consider them very primitive and say, "Surely they have progressed beyond that?". But for those particular people their customs and habits are satisfactory, because they are suited to their particular degree of progress.

If you find yourself rejecting anything, it will be either because you are not ready to receive it or you have gone beyond it. Either way, do not let it distress you or in any way diminish your own convictions or your own beliefs, if such afford you comfort and give you a responsive ring of truth within yourself.

I can only solemnly swear to you that, as a messenger of the spirit world on the level to which I belong, these have been my experiences.

ARRIVAL ON THE ASTRAL PLANE

BEFORE discussing the actual transition and what occurs when a spirit enters the spirit world, it should be emphasised that the physical conditions prior to the passing are of quite considerable importance in relation to the mental awakening of the new life.

For instance, in the case of an elderly man who has lived a good long life upon the earth plane and whose physical body has deteriorated naturally, his spirit may leave the body quite often prior to the actual severance of the silver cord. You know that it is the severance of this cord that separates the spirit entirely from the physical body. Once that has happened the body is indeed dead.

During periods of sleep or unconsciousness which often precede a transition, the spirit makes journeys while the silver cord which links the spirit body to the physical gradually becomes thinner and thinner. On these journeys, the soul has made acquaintance with those who are waiting to receive him finally, and so he is gradually prepared for his awakening. While this slow and gentle separation is taking place, he may return to physical consciousness and remark that during his "dream" he saw and spoke to his mother, father or wife. This, of course, is not a dream but a spiritual experience and part of the preparation for the passing. So when the body is finally severed from the spirit, it is a natural thing for the spirit to feel that he is still dreaming, and to enjoy this experience without fear or any sense of shock.

It must be emphasised that your arrival into Spirit has nothing whatever to do with your subsequent spiritual status. You are not yet awakened to the realisation of your own particular point of progression; that progression which will ultimately determine where you belong in Spirit. This comes afterwards. The state of the spirit on arrival is much coarser than it subsequently will become. As it has been only recently released, its vibrations are still temporarily allied to those of the physical body. This is applicable in all cases, whatever the conditions of passing.

Now, we must consider the case of a person who passes through a sudden or tragic death.

The victim of an accident is totally unaware of what has happened to him because the ejection of the spirit, the severance of the cord, is so sudden that the sense of shock is that which he associates with the accident. He is quite prepared to declare that he is not hurt, that he is "perfectly all right". This is the first reaction, because he thinks he has had a miraculous escape. He still mentally accepts himself as he was; so, to himself, he looks precisely the same.

This "spiritual dressing" is an entirely mental factor. Clothes are created by the recollection of what you think you should be wearing. That is why, when spirits who have lived in Victorian or Edwardian times return, they do so in the clothes of those eras. By remembering themselves as they were, they create those clothes over their spirit. They do not wear them in their own spiritual homes, but their recollection is allied to them, so they adopt them for the purpose of recognition. In the same way, in the case of a sudden passing, there is a mental picture of the clothing the person was wearing at the time of the accident. To himself, therefore, he looks exactly the same as he was a few moments before.

So this spirit suddenly ejected from the body tries hard to reassure those who were around him when he passed that he is "all right", but he finds that he can make no impression on them.

But, close to him, though possibly unseen, are those friends in Spirit who have come to meet him; for while he would have had no prior knowledge of his own death, the spirit helpers would have been well informed and ready for this entry into Spirit. But their contact with this soul is dependent upon the mental effort made by him to receive some sort of enlightenment or help in his bewilderment.

The newly arrived spirit sees what appears to be his own body, though he cannot understand it, for here he is, perfectly well and in one piece. But, as soon as he acknowledges, "There is something odd about this, I wish I knew more about it", his mind is able to receive the help that is awaiting him.

The spirit helpers will try, first, to lead him away from the scene of the accident, for by remaining close to these emotional sensations he can become too strongly involved and so shut out the help that is waiting to be given. Alternatively, they might try to explain to him what has happened to his body.

Sometimes this is premature, but the helpers generally know from experience whether trying to explain what has happened will be of avail or whether he is not yet ready for the explanation. His response to this effort is dependent upon his mental receptivity. This is impossible to classify since no one can truly assess the mental reaction of another. So they might say to him: "Don't worry. Come along with us and we will take you somewhere where you can recover from the shock". And because most people are frightened by the unusual, he would probably grasp at this offer of help.

He would be taken to a place that closely resembles a hospital reception centre, for the mind vaguely anticipates some such place. This familiar atmosphere plays its part in establishing confidence and allaying fears and doubts. He might ask for, and receive, a cigarette or a cup of tea; everything appears quite normal and very closely allied to the world that is left behind.

All this takes place in the astral belt of communication. From our side it is not dark but rather like a thick, white mist. As we vibrate into it, we become invisible from the spiritual side of things, but are able to see physical things quite normally. It is on this astral belt that the Spirit is received and assisted by what may be termed "spiritual first-aid".

You will see that the circumstances of the passing play a

tremendous part in these early moments of reception on the Other Side. It is not necessary to know that you have died, but your mental faculties must be receptive. You have to recognise that something has happened to you and you need help. There are many who do not realise that there has been any change whatsoever, and for them it is a constant repetition of trying to impress people upon earth that they are still there. These efforts to communicate do not necessarily exclude the possibility of spiritual help for them.

It frequently happens that when a person is described by a medium at a clairvoyant demonstration, the recipient says, "But he is not yet buried," or "The funeral service is tomorrow". This almost invariably takes place before the visit of the spirit to his spirit home.

The spirit would be concerned about those whom he loved. Very often we, the guides, who are always present on these occasions, find the one who has just come over is totally unwilling to leave the vicinity of his recently vacated body until all the funeral arrangements are over. It all depends on how important to the spirit are those he has left behind, and how deeply distressed they are.

But when your spirit friend communicates with you at a later period he will do so from his spiritual home, and will not be nearly so coarse, so dense in his makeup as in the immediate passing days. This is why some of you say, "I saw my mother the first week that she passed, but now I do not see her". This is because the spirit has increased her rate of vibration so that she is not so dense, and therefore not nearly so visible to you.

Those who have sincerely believed that death is a long sleep which will only be ended when the "trumpet sounds", *will* sleep, and will continue to do so until they themselves are spiritually ready to be enlightened. Many years may elapse before this stage is reached, though every effort is made during their periodical returns to consciousness to enlighten them as to their true state.

Perhaps the most common case is that of a newly arrived soul, who, whilst having no knowledge of spirit return, is convinced of Survival, without any clear idea of what to expect in the next state. Gradually, he has been weaned away from the earthly emotional plane he has so recently left behind, and is now able to see quite clearly and as solidly as you in the body see each other. We are solid to each other; we are not so to you, simply because we are on a different rate of vibration. There is nothing ethereal or unsubstantial about this relationship that we bear to one another.

In the joy and happiness of reunion, perspectives change. The long, lonely years of separation from dear ones pass quickly from the mind, and it awakens a new spiritual consciousness; the mind is flooded with memories of spiritual experiences which were buried deep during life in the physical body. Conversations and meetings that occurred during the sleep state or during periods of release from the body are vividly remembered. There are no long gaps to be filled in, for with true spiritual association there is no break. It is only those associations that are true and real that are able to endure in this spiritual sense.

You may desire to stay among familiar surroundings, such as houses and places where, in your recollections, you have been happy and comfortable. This depends entirely upon how reliant you were upon these material things while in the physical body. If you think of things as necessities, then you will take longer to break free from them. There is no harm in this - after all, you have all Eternity. Most of your friends can meet you there; some are still enjoying such physical recollections themselves. Many retain this recollection because they are not yet separate from it, so on this astral belt they still have the counterpart of the little thatched cottage or the house they always wanted by the sea.

This astral belt has perhaps a little finer, a little lighter vibrations than those immediately surrounding the earth, but they are only of vibrations, not places as such. All the trained guide has to do is to learn to control and regulate them.

As you go towards your spirit home, you will quicken your vibration - not sufficiently to be in your real spirit home as yet, but sufficiently to separate yourself from what we call the emotional astral vibration that is closest to the earth. With this separation, too, will go a great many of your unpleasant recollections, because your mind is now full of the joy of your dear ones and the beauty of the home that is waiting for you. This home, incidentally, is the product of your mental desires.

Your own thought waves are moulded by your friends into something tangible and real and solid, subject to your right to it. You cannot fulfil your dreams and hopes without the spiritual right to enjoy them. This depends upon the faithfulness with which you have grasped the opportunities that life has offered you by way of service to others.

This brings me to the next stage. In your busy physical earth lives you must often say, "Surely there must be something to do there". This again depends on your mental desires.

It is important here to realise that it is necessary for you to enjoy everything you have felt the need of in the physical body before you can leave behind this particular earthly cycle. Yet this is not the entirety of your experience; it is only a particular physical experience through which you have recently passed. But everything allied to that by way of desire must be enjoyed and fulfilled. So this is what happens. You discover many things in yourself of which you were not aware, and, much more important, you are now able to expand. Perhaps you have always longed to play the piano? Then here you will do so and express yourself musically in a way that satisfies what was always a desperate hunger whilst you were on the earth plane.

Here is another important point. If your mind cannot conceive being able to play the piano without first learning in the accepted sense then, indeed, you will go through the processes of learning. But, if you are mentally alive to this creative power within yourself then you will be able to sit down and play without any of the tedium of learning. It is entirely dependent upon your own mental approach.

So, if you look now at the gaps in your life, you can see that these unfulfilled desires will provide ample occupation for you.

This particular phase of existence takes no account of the sort of job you have made of your life. It simply helps you to separate yourself from physical recollection. It is a very happy state, and necessary to most people, because, good or bad, we have always to recuperate spiritual strength. Most of us are in need of this period during which we can "get our breath back" and sort ourselves out.

But this state of existence is not your true spirit home. When your mental freedom has enabled you to release yourself from all the ties of physical recollection and leave only the spiritual implication of that experience, when that time comes you will be in a position to draw away from this astral belt and proceed to your real spiritual home. This could be either "up" or "down" according to your spiritual status.

So it is this varied spiritual home that brings you in touch with people. And this is a happy thought: you contact only those with whom you feel this warm, harmonious sympathy, only those who are on your wavelength, because this is part of your mental restoration.

The length of time that friends are able to remain with you in this spirit home is largely dependent upon the depths and strength of their love for you and yours for them, and also upon their willingness, prompted by that love, to remain with you.

In my own experience, I have never met two people, or groups of people, if you like, that have been truly devoted to each other whilst on the earth plane, one of whom has ever wanted to go on before the object of his devotion joined him. They willingly wait because by waiting here they are accessible to those on the earth even though often this wonderful spiritual relationship is unknown to the physical consciousness of the loved one left behind. Nonetheless, the one waiting in Spirit, whose love is so great and so powerful, is sustained and fortified by the many thoughts of loving recollection that reach him so constantly from the one left behind.

What happens after this is solely dependent upon what you have done with the physical responsibilities that life has presented. But, again, you are rarely separated from your dear ones, for, while it cannot be a foregone conclusion that you can remain with them - this depending upon your own spiritual development - nonetheless because their love is so great, they may choose to remain with you.

This always provides a greater impetus for the struggling spirit to reach out from the abyss in which, perhaps, its own neglect, thoughtlessness or selfishness has placed it. If you know that somebody whom you dearly love is on your account in surroundings that are far less pleasant than he or she deserves, you will work much harder to get out of that condition, so that your love may find release in your promotion. But, remember, there is no conventional pattern here, no sentimental acceptance of a devotion that is solely identified with lip service. Friendship must be genuine or it is non-existent.

If you can conceive a life without all the pin-pricks and notes of disharmony that you now have to encounter, if you can imagine meeting only the people with whom you feel in complete rapport, if you can imagine a world where you are able to express yourself in all the unattainable ways for which your spirit has yearned, then this is the place to which you can look forward upon your arrival.

It has to be individual. Your pleasure and upliftment need not necessarily be mine. We enjoy, of course, totally different friends and have around us totally different relations. But for both of us it would remain a place of complete fulfilment and happiness.

Have you ever experienced a moment of complete happiness? If you can recapture that moment and say, "Then I was truly happy - then everything was right", and extend it, you have some idea what this Paradise may be.

You will find this Paradise an essentially individual thing, but you do not have to worry about disturbing anybody or about anyone getting in your way. There is all the space you need. You are creating your own atmosphere of realisation. Everything will be solid, everything will be real. Should you want a change in your home or surroundings you think them all different, and there they are around you without any of the customary labour. Inconceivable but true!

This is what we mean by fulfilling all your longings and dreams. You will find that the gratification of your desires quickly palls, but at least you have the pleasure of it before this happens. Here there are no rules or regulations - simply the integral relationships of spiritual unity that result in companion-ship and association with all those spiritual beings who will be just as anxious to be close to you as you are to be close to them.

No, it does not last. It is not meant to. But you will have it as long as you want it. Nobody will hurry you. Nobody will say it is time to get started and you ought to be doing this or that. You yourself will be sated with it first, and then you will say in effect, "I am ready now, ready to face up to what lies ahead of me, to recognise what I have to do to bring myself nearer to God's heart". This was, in essence, the purpose of the physical experience through which you have passed.

HEAVEN AND HELL

OUR talk tonight is entitled "Heaven and Hell" but in effect it is a continuation of the subject we were discussing last time, which was the interim period that occurs when you first enter the spirit world.

As I mentioned, in this interim period you were, so to speak, finding your feet in a new form of consciousness. You greeted your friends, you experienced the fulfilment of your desires, whether they were physical or spiritual in their implication, and enjoyed the beauties of what is known as the "Summerland".

Gradually you began to shed the memories of the experiences you went through in your earth life and began the process of becoming "spiritually whole" by also taking into account other experiences, which you had undergone in previous lives. You could not, of course, realise fully this "wholeness" until you shed and forgot the physical memories of your last life.

As you did this and awakened to a realisation of your true spiritual identity, you became aware of all the imperfections of your last life and all the opportunities you lost.

Now, at this moment while you are still in the body, there is only a small part of your spiritual consciousness functioning. You have only that measure of spiritual supervision, in terms of influence and direction, that is relevant and necessary to the experiences of the life that you are living. You have much dormant authority - spiritual authority within you. You have a reservoir of strength pertaining to that identity upon which you draw, but you can draw only to the extent that is necessary to your needs during this particular lifetime.

You have heard me many times liken the experiences of life to the polishing of one facet of a diamond. And if you consider a diamond with hundreds of facets, then the particular phase of life through which you are now passing is but one of those facets. If you can accept, by the same analogy, that the many or the few lives you have experienced in the past are a shining part of that diamond, then you have still a part of your diamond that is untried and unpolished, and this we could equate with lives or experiences still to come. In short, we have those facets that you have experienced and have taken to their final perfection through both physical and subsequent spiritual experience, and we have this facet with which we are engaged now at this particular time.

You can therefore draw the light of this diamond as far as it is polished on those facets that have been perfected; you can draw the light of those facets, but the facet on which you are now working is quite separate.

Now hold this analogy of the diamond in your mind, because it will help you to understand what I am talking about when I deal with levels of thought and consciousness that are completely separate from your physical experiences here on earth. I shall try to illustrate by examples the true meaning of what I am striving to express and explain, but none of these examples, dear friends, will be really adequate since we are dealing in our present discussion with a totally different dimension from your physical one. There are laws and experiences, emotional impacts and levels of consciousness that are in your present inhibited state totally foreign to you. So you must accept the limitations of both the explanations and your ability to understand them.

As I have said, we have now reached the stage in your spirit life when you have shed your earth memories and passed through the interim period, and where you have begun to enter the state of spiritual wholeness. You can now to a certain extent measure a little of your success or failure in polishing the diamond

diamond in your most recent incarnation.

Now, almost without exception, we become aware of various shortcomings and flaws. We are aware of this not with regard to particular incidents. We do not say: "If only I had been kinder to my mother! If only I had been more considerate to my wife! If only I had not withheld my help when my son asked for it!".

We do not measure in physical detail; you must remember that you have passed beyond physical appreciation of things. Indeed, in your earth lives, while you saw the reason and aim of your purpose in spiritual terms and were shown a reasonably accurate pattern that you were to follow in order to achieve your spiritual objective, the detail was always secondary to the spiritual itself. You are now in your new spirit life confronted with the spiritual implications both of your successes and failures.

A lot of people are confused when we talk about this, because they believe that some of their imperfections and shortcomings are inherited from previous lives, but to my knowledge this is not so.

As we return to that "spiritual wholeness" we bring with us imperfections, jobs not very well done, many a neglected duty, and so on. We have entered the spirit world with a lot of imperfections, a lot of flaws in the particular facet that we have been endeavouring to polish.

This is why it is so important for you to have a clear understanding of the Law of Survival and the reality of the spirit world, as it will help you to cure or lessen your imperfections and neglectful habits while you are still in the body.

This is the reason why I am trying to explain these things to you in the hope that you may be more fortunate than I was in recognising, while still in the body, the importance of integrity and conscientious application in everything you do.

So, to return to our spirit world and my own experience. I have gone through what you call the Summerland, I have forgotten my own Chinese existence and have come now to the realisation of my true spiritual identity.

To explain this to you I must first of all define what I mean by "spiritual wholeness". Have you ever had the experience where you have been completely conscious, aware of yourself, and yet have been unaware of your surroundings, when your environment means nothing to you whatsoever?

This is a fairly common experience in people who have not long to live, because they can and do separate themselves from their physical consciousness. They become immediately aware of a fountain of spiritual strength and power that is enabling them to effect a separation from their physical body.

You may already have experienced this feeling of separateness on an occasion when you were so ill that you were not expected to live. It is not separation in any callous or careless sense, but a complete disregard, a feeling of complete serenity and peace, with no concern for anything, or awareness of people around you, with all the emotional impact removed. This very inadequately describes the sensation or awareness of this "spiritual wholeness". You are not a person in any physical sense; you are supported by something that is almost unidentifiable, you have lost your own identity without any concern or anxiety about it.

This stage of consciousness is what the spirit people call "floating out". It is a kind of emerging from the pull and pressure of the physical into a true spiritual release, and for a little while you don't really know where you are, you don't recognise people around you and you are not concerned at all. There is no feeling of distress. It is a kind of oblivion, but a conscious oblivion.

Then you become aware - and remember I am speaking of my own personal experience - of what I can only describe as a harmonic reverberation around you, a beautiful ecstasy, which is impossible for me to put into words.

But if you can imagine yourself being wholly part of wonderful music, wonderful painting, wonderful colour and vistas of nature, this is the sensation. You feel this divine, ecstatic, unified power with such indescribable joy that you just don't know what is happening to you.

There is music and laughter, there is love, there is every quality that is of the highest and best, and your spirit responds to it. This, I suppose, is the true definition of Heaven. Heaven is not in beautiful surroundings, although, of course, that is possible. Heaven is not being surrounded by people we love, although that is part of it. Heaven, real Heaven, is this indescribable unity with a divine whole that is joy and upliftment beyond description.

I cannot explain it to you any further than that, but as I try to make these words convey something, I hope you can feel yourselves lifted up. I can feel the highest and best in you spiritually receiving this element of harmony that I am trying to explain.

If you could take the highest and best experience in your life and multiply it millions and billions of times, this would give you some idea of the joy of this spiritual wholeness. It is true harmony. You feel it rushing towards you, pouring through you. You are part of it. Swept up in it you revel in it - all the healing, all the love, all the compassion, forgiveness and mercy, all the grace.

There is no time in this kind of experience. Indeed there is no time as such in the spirit life, no time as you understand the word. But one is limited to a certain extent by one's imperfections in one's capacity to enjoy. You enjoy this ecstasy because of those things you have done well, those things in which you have been faithful, loyal and true to yourself. The more faithfully you have fulfilled your duty here on earth so far as you knew it, the more you are able to enjoy this level of perfection.

In my own case, I found myself in this ecstatic state aware of people around me. They were not the people I had known in my earthly life, for I had lost that physical memory. The people around me were people from whom I knew I had never been separated. It is important to note this, for husband and wife are not necessarily spiritual companions: brother and sister, mother and daughter, father and son are not necessarily spiritual affinities.

They are people who have agreed to walk together on the physical pathway. So, when this complete separation from the earth life takes place, you will have forgotten about them as people. But, if they are for you, you will know them in their "spiritual wholeness", and this will contain all the love, all the joy, all the experiences you have shared together in a previous or perhaps many previous lives.

There is no relationship as such in this fellowship. In this spiritual family there are only souls responding to souls, and these harmonise as pieces of an orchestra harmonise.

So, in part, this Heaven consists in meeting our own. There is a lovely old hymn which describes this meeting, "We shall know as we are known". It is a recognition of spiritual compatibility with those who travel with us through all Eternity.

We are always attached to our particular spiritual group. Sometimes they walk beside us in the physical experiences of our earth life. Sometimes they act as spiritual guardians and help us on the way. Sometimes they act as guides as I am a guide to this particular instrument (Ivy Northage). But it does not necessarily follow that because the guide is using a particular instrument he and the instrument are spiritually related or united, although it can be so.

So, this further extension of Heaven consists in recognising kindred souls, in sharing this zenith, this highest possible experience of love that we can know. Naturally, the more progressed we are, the higher we have travelled on the ladder of divine progress, the more complete, the more joyous is our ecstasy. We find ourselves, then, as I found myself, among those dear beloved friends with whom we have everything in common and whom we meet in a divine fellowship.

Here again also you experience activity, but it is so completely different from your physical activity that it is difficult for me to give an example without confusing you. If you can imagine doing all the things you want to do and if you can imagine the joy, if you are a creative person, that you have found in composing a piece of music, writing a poem, painting a picture or even losing yourself in the power of thought that takes you beyond the limitation of physical things, then that is something like the activity of which I am speaking.

I do not mean painting, music and poetry as such. I mean the release, the spiritual release and fulfilment that it represents. For this spiritual heaven is a creative heaven, but it is not creative in the sense that you understand creation in your earth life. We do not make things with our hands or mould things or write things. We develop this activity out of our love for one another, and through that love we are directed towards an activity that is relative to the spiritual experience of which we are a part, and all this experience partakes of the same harmony. We cannot on this level do anything that is irksome or difficult or which provides us with any kind of problem.

Everything that we do is subject to a harmonic unity. We do everything together and share a common love and joy in everything that we do. I suppose that one of the greatest trials of those who are travelling the spiritual path on earth is the increasing feeling of loneliness and separation from people around them. For as we progress we try to understand spiritual laws and to put them into practice. As a consequence we seem to be more and more misunderstood and ostracised by those around us, by people who are not necessarily unkind or cruel, but with whom we have nothing in common.

Now reverse this picture. Instead of getting further and further away from people, imagine that every moment you are meeting more and more spiritual friends and getting closer to them. Imagine, too, that the joy, ecstasy and upliftment that this brings is one that you share together, so that it is all increased one hundred fold! That is the beautiful and lovely side - a divine and merciful compassion - and there is nothing harsh about the judgement and punishment that follows this kind of ecstasy, since both judgement and punishment are self imposed.

No one judges you, no one punishes you: there is nobody standing by to do these things to you. You do them yourself of your own free will, because as you have gradually absorbed into yourself the reward - reward, indeed, is a misleading term though it represents as nearly as possible what I want to say, for there is no reward as such, there is only goodness for goodness' sake, goodness is reward in itself because it brings us into this unity with the God Force - you experience this unity to the fullest extent of your capacity to realise and appreciate what it entails. The extent of your capacity for this appreciation is measured by and is the result of the laws you have obeyed, your integrity and your faithfulness, and you absorb and enjoy it to the level to which you are entitled.

But gradually you become aware of a discordant note. This does not come over very powerfully at first, but it would seem as if these dearly loved and new-found friends are a little further away. There is a sadness that creeps into your consciousness; somehow or other it seems as if a cloud were passing over the face of the sun. You feel a little uncomfortable and, because of the high level of appreciation that this state of spiritual consciousness demands, you are increasingly pained by this sense of discord.

You begin to feel the most frightful anguish within yourself. It is something like a physical pain, but is very hard to define. I think the legend - and it is merely a legend - of the Garden of Eden depicts something of this, inasmuch as Adam and Eve enjoyed a wonderful state of happiness and ecstasy, which was replaced by an awful desolation, when they sinned and were driven out of the garden.

So, I was aware of a most frightful desolate anguish within myself, which was all the greater because of the wonderful and really indescribable happiness and upliftment that I had so recently been enjoying. This desolation was like a dreadful earthquake which had robbed me of everything I had known and loved. I felt utterly alone.

The great majority of people are ordinary, everyday persons who do their best. There are comparatively few really evil people, but such as there are have to go through the full extent of their evil-doing. The greatest crime is to set out deliberately to hurt and victimise others, particularly the helpless, particularly those who are unable to defend themselves. I am not going to describe to you the kind of experiences these people pass through. It is sufficient to say it is invariably absolute darkness; they themselves have shut out God's Light by their own inhumanity to fellow beings.

Remember there are degrees of this, and what may seem to you a vile and terrible crime may not, in spiritual terms, be nearly so bad as it appears to you. Conversely, those who seem to you to have done not so much damage may be infinitely worse in spiritual terms. So, do not try to judge or assess degrees of evil- doing. Just accept that life is offering you opportunities whereby you can serve your fellow men. Nobody who understands spiritual law expects you to go rushing here, there and everywhere looking for opportunities. All you are asked to do is to seize and fulfil faithfully the opportunities that come to you.

Let us suppose these opportunities place you in a position of power, in a position which enables you to make happy or unhappy the conditions of people who are quite helpless, and that you exploit your power and use it for your own ends with complete disregard to whatever suffering you may cause. If you do this, you are creating for yourself the worst kind of Hell it is possible to experience.

The worst thing we can do is to tyrannise over and cause suffering to others. Hell is inescapable. Nobody condemns you or seizes you and pushes you into this Hell. Nobody, however much they love you, can release you from it until you yourself have done something to mitigate or atone for the effects of those actions that have brought you there. There can be no release from this state except by your own actions. To make reparation or atonement in the spiritual state is much more difficult than it was when you were on the earth plane. As I have said and must repeat, there is no crime worse than to set out deliberately to harm or hurt another fellow human being.

We do a lot of things thoughtlessly, we do a lot of things that are misunderstood, we hurt people without realising we have done so. These cases come into an entirely different category and may be classed under the heading of imperfections, inasmuch as we ought by spiritual law to be more spiritually perceptive and aware of the needs and feelings of those around us.

But this is quite different from deliberately setting out to trample on another. You must also realise there are degrees and levels in the Hell which people suffer, who have been guilty of cruelty to their fellow men. I am not going to dwell unduly upon this, because the people who are guilty of this sort of crime are in the minority. But believe me there is not one of us who can escape one hair's breadth of retribution for anything we have done.

Although I have talked about the really evil being in total darkness, the exquisite torture of those of us who are more advanced is quite relative to the darkness and dreadful conditions through which the more definitely evil people pass. These sufferings are comparative. As you progress, your degree of ecstasy and joy is increased, but so also is the result of your imperfections.

To return once more to my own experience, as I have said, I was aware of the most frightful desolation. After all the joy and light and colour and love, it was as if I was suddenly surrounded by twilight, and I called out for help. "What has happened? Where am I?" And immediately my particular guides were there. But they were quite detached as they explained to me that I was now experiencing the imperfections of my most recent life or facet, and how these imperfections separated me from Divine unity. Of course I could not appreciate this until I saw exactly what these imperfections were.

I was shown this by being taken to a place, quite alone, which was very like a life-size television screen. On it I was shown from beginning to end the whole of my most recent life, every shade and every nuance of experience, the results of my thoughts and neglects, and all the people these things had affected. Thus, if you are rude, short tempered with a shop assistant, to somebody on the way, they in turn become annoyed, are unkind to somebody else and so the sequence goes on. And, because you started it, you bear the brunt of that particular set of circumstances, everything magnified, everything multiplied in its effect upon each one. Dear friends, you cannot conceive anything more painful and utterly desolating!

However, you forget about this immediately you have redeemed yourself, unless you have reason, as I have reason now, to remember these things in order to talk to you. But I no longer feel the pain. It is rather like looking up the Akashic Records. I am able to turn over the page and refer to these experiences rather than to go through them all over again. At first I could not talk about them to others and nobody shared them, for they were entirely personal. Most people have to sit through this record of their lives two or three times, because they cannot take it all at once. As you become more evolved this repetition becomes less necessary, but I think I sat through mine three or four times.

How can I tell you or describe my sensations during that frightful ordeal? Imagine yourself drenched with cold perspiration and feeling that horrible sensation that fear brings. So, I think, would most people be affected. Everything was shown to me and I saw how easily I could have avoided this or that, how simple it would have been to hold out a helping hand here or there, how easy it would have been if I had made myself find time for that! I wanted to weep and could not.

I had no means of expressing my most frightful anguish or the terrible feeling with which I watched my crimes, for they looked like crimes in that intensified appreciation that is relative to spiritual wholeness. I watched and I watched! You do not get any mitigation. You cannot say, "True, I did all those things but, after all, I did a bit of good here and a kindly act there." You cannot draw comfort from these actions, because you have already drawn credit for them in the joy, happiness and unity that you previously experienced. You are like a person who suffers from shell shock, and in this very chastened state you are taken to what they call the Halls of Healing.

In certain circumstances you may be crippled by peoples' behaviour towards you, but this can only happen when you have not learned to forgive. If you carry resentment in your heart, you will see that resentment and see what it has done to you. I was not affected in this way, because although I had many imperfections, I had no resentment, as I had expiated this in my last life. Nevertheless, I had no identity, I had no power in myself. I was trembling and very frightened; you know how fear paralyses you and how sufferings and torture can take away all your will - everything that helps you to recognise yourself as a person.

If you can imagine this, you will realise the state I was in when I had finished reviewing my past life. I could not walk and had to be carried. For although we can glide, hover or move with the speed of thought on the plane to which we belong, and do not have your limitations, our spirit world is nevertheless solid to us and we often walk around, just as you do.

Well, now I could not walk. I was too weak and was therefore carried or supported by my guardians, who took me to a Hall of Healing. I do not think I slept in the physical sense but was in a kind of oblivion. The spiritual skin which had been torn away by my recent experience gradually reformed and I was made whole, rather like burned skin being replaced. For I had been literally stripped by the experience and left defenceless.

During this period of oblivion and healing you are aware of people talking to you and advising you. First of all you have to seek forgiveness from all those whom you have harmed. These people, like yourself, are not always ready to give you this because they still have to progress. It is not just a question of saying: "I am terribly sorry. What can I do to put it right?".

You have to receive the forgiveness of those whom you have harmed. And in this state of oblivion, it is as though you were talking to these people. They are not present with you, but your mind is in touch with their minds and you are speaking to them - acknowledging that you pained them in this way or that. "Can you bring yourself to forgive me?" you ask. And if they can, you are indeed fortunate, because that particular shortcoming has been healed in love and your debt has been paid.

All this you will find in the parables of the New Testament. You remember about Jesus talking of the person who owed so much and the person who owed little, and how much greater was the compassion, the mercy of the one who forgave much. But you cannot do anything further until you have received the forgiveness of those whom you have harmed. This may or may not be given to you; it depends entirely upon their spiritual progression. This forgiveness is for them a means of progression and you in turn have people to forgive. This interchange is the next step in this particular experience of what is still to pay.

You have either received forgiveness or been refused it. If it has been refused you still have to bear the pain of that particular imperfection and it is a pain. But there is an injection of love from those who have forgiven you and found it in their hearts to do so with complete generosity and love.

When all this has been dealt with, you are now brought back to spiritual consciousness and greater strength. You are now very chastened and have forgotten the experience of love and light that your Heaven represented. That has been completely cut off for the time being, and you don't have its comfort. You are on your own; you know you are the only person who can do anything about it. You have plenty of advisers and counsellors, but they are external and can only give advice. You yourself have to expiate, must do all by yourself what you have been advised to do.

Always, dear friends, when your strength fails you, and it will fail you many times, you are taken to the Hall of Healing again and you are put into oblivion in order that you may gradually increase your strength. There is nothing merciless or harsh about this. Every time you make the effort, you make the effort by yourself. There is no one to help, no one to do it for you.

To return to my own experience, let us say I had been forgiven by those in the spirit world whom I had harmed, and I in turn had offered my forgiveness to those who had injured me, thereby mitigating and expiating many of my own shortcomings and neglects. But there were still people upon the earth plane whom I had harmed by my attitude and who had not yet followed me into the spirit world.

The saying that the sins of the fathers are visited upon the children not only means physical diseases; it has a spiritual implication. If I had harmed a father and his child suffered in consequence, then my debt is to the child who is still upon the earth plane and to his son and grandson, if what I had done affected them in the slightest degree. So there were those I had left behind, whom I had harmed in this thoughtless and selfish way, and I had to deal with this problem. It was not any good asking their forgiveness, because they did not understand. So I had to find a way to pay my debt directly to them.

This explains why we work so hard and diligently to try to bring enlightenment and understanding to you, while you are still in your earth life. It is by trying with diligent, loyal and faithful service to prevent you from falling into the pitfalls that we have fallen into that we are able to save you from making the same mistakes.

I had to come into the Astral and was taught how to hang about there - there is no other word for it - and try to get my thoughts to the person whom I had wronged or who had been subsequently affected by my actions. I had to try to get them to respond to the help I was offering them.

Every time they found life too hard and every time my strength and power reached them, something of my faults was washed away. So, because only to the extent of the debts that we owe are we expected to respond, gradually the debts were paid. Here, there was no question of forgiveness being withheld, because the persons concerned did not know, so I had to rely upon their ability to take my help and to act upon it, which can only be done through their aura.

So you can see what a hard, uphill journey this returning to spiritual perfection can be. Gradually I paid my debts and gradually I was restored because, as these imperfections became less and less, as the debts became reduced to a minimum, so the spiritual light of love and fellowship began to pour back into me and I was restored. It is rather like your parable of the Prodigal Son and the Father waiting to welcome, rejoice and be happy, because of your return home.

This then, dear friends, is Heaven and Hell, but always remember that nobody can carry your load of sin, nobody can expiate your crimes except you yourself. It is you who have to do it and nobody else.

If you are fortunate in that those you have wronged are spiritually awakened so that they are able to forgive, you are indeed fortunate; but even so, there will be certain repercussions over which they have no power or control, and these you must bear for yourselves.

So, we have come full cycle. We have entered the spirit world, we have met and enjoyed our friends and loved ones, we have experienced to the full the material desires and aspirations denied us on the earth plane. We have realised our true spiritual stature and experienced the harmony and happiness this represents. And, as we entered into this full realisation of our true identity, we became aware of the blots and blemishes that demanded the cleansing of redemption. Now, we re-enter this state of perfect Bliss to enjoy what this last incarnation has earned us in terms of spiritual at-onement. What happens now I hope to speak of in our next lecture.

MANY MANSIONS

MANY Mansions, in terms of spiritual evolvement, is a coming home to the heart of God and a divine perfection to the level of your ability to appreciate and reflect it.

We are now with a state of consciousness that has no physical comparison, wherein you are completely released from all that this present incarnation represents and restored to your spiritual identity. When you enter the earth plane you bring with you a small facet of your spiritual wholeness. Although you have access to the reservoir of that wholeness, you can only effectively understand and use a small part of it.

The same thing applies to a lesser degree in my ministry. I return from a spiritual home to control an instrument in this way. In so doing I limit my capacity of spiritual wholeness by way of expression. Very often I cannot understand enough in this state to explain things to you that belong to my full range of consciousness. So I have to limit what I am able to tell you in the same way that you are limited in your understanding. As spirits you are much more advanced than you are able to understand whilst occupying the physical body.

When you enter the spirit world, gradually you are able to shed what memory would have you hold on to. People are judged by the things they value most. If these things are solely physical, your subsequent release from the probationary or intermediary period in the spirit world will be much more prolonged because your interests, your love and your heart have been directed towards things of a physical nature. When you are deeply concerned with things of the earth, it is much harder to leave them behind.

Conversely, if you have sought only spiritual values, if the actual material pattern of your life has been, so to speak, the uniform that you wear in applying yourself to this spiritual purpose, then for you the memory of such values and pleasures will be short. As the butterfly shakes off the chrysalis, so you will very quickly shake off these memories, and you will become a whole spirit.

In this spiritual existence we still have shape and form, but it has no bearing on physiognomy or appearance. A spirit is recognised by the radiance that shines from the face. The form of a spirit is rather like a face draped in light. There is nothing ethereal or insubstantial about it - it has its own solidity, but only upon its own level. It does not require shape in the way you know the term.

Think of countless millions of souls who have passed through various incarnations. Each incarnation is a kind of appendage to your spiritual personality and identity. This appendage is moulded by the opportunities that you have accepted and dealt with. It is a means of enlarging yourself spiritually.

There are appendages of light and darkness, the light being spiritual attainment and the darkness neglected opportunities and wasted effort. "Hell" is a means of eradicating the darkness and causing it to come to be at one with the light. As this occurs, you are gradually able to absorb this darkness so that it becomes less and less and you become spiritually bigger. You don't grow taller and wider; you grow lighter. Everything to do with spiritual attainment is reflected in light and purification.

Here, in this state of Many Mansions you have no mixing with people who are outside your range. You have graduated to your own spiritual level and are now entirely with your own spiritual family. This creates the spiritual identity to which you belong and entitles you to what we are going to call your Spiritual Mansion.

It is not a house as such, but obviously on the level with your ability to understand and appreciate. You have places to which you resort which bring out the uttermost joy in you. Try to imagine this in terms of silent understanding one with another. You know that wonderful sense of joy; to be with somebody and not have to speak to explain what you mean because they understand. Now, this is a very crude analogy, but you are on the right lines if you can multiply it hundreds of times. Think of Many Mansions, not as a standard of appreciation of painting, decor, music, entertainment, but as a range of spiritual attunement, and the range is important.

Jesus told his disciples that he was going to prepare a place for them. He explained that he was going on ahead, and that there were places for all kinds of people in the spiritual home to which he was going.

This spiritual state has nothing to do with the level from which your own dear ones can return to you, for when you reach this level you have finished with the physical or spirit world as you know it. But you are not leaving behind anything that you still love, for were you still in love with the person or conditions relative to that most recent physical experience, you would not leave it behind. You cannot have that kind of longing in this spiritual home; you have spent it, you have already enjoyed it.

You can think now in terms of appreciation of people who instructed or helped you. "I didn't want to learn that, but now I realise how valuable was the teaching." You look back in terms of this rather abstract appreciation without the detail or memory of a particular incident that it would represent.

There is no sense of regret because you have now reaped and garnered the value of the experience in spiritual terms. Your capacity for joy and true affinity with God is accentuated and multiplied by it.

This goes out from you in a kind of radiance that gives you a personal label, and you are known by the colour that you are able to emit. Spiritually now you have perfected yourself to the level of attainment that you have reached; you are a pure Whole and have gone to the spiritual mansion that represents. It is a state of being that brings you into harmony and loving participation with everything that is in keeping with your own inclination and aspirations. This spiritual fulfilment not only gives you the beauty and wonderful experience of enjoying the highest and best in yourself, but it shows you your potential for the next step.

It does not show you something in the clouds which says that if you go back to the earth plane and work hard and suffer all over again you will get up here, but you are brought into touch with people who are on the next rung of your spiritual ladder. You see them in their perfected state, and something of you is pulled like a magnet towards that further attainment. There is the most exquisite love in all this. You are surrounded by it in a sense that you cannot understand in physical terms. But if you can attune your highest moment of ecstasy and at-onement with another person and your surroundings, this is the kind of love to which I refer.

So, you are surrounded by your own people in this lovely state of ecstatic perfection, and also by those who have gone just that step ahead and who will create in you, not an envious longing, not an aching desire, but a genuine love that causes you to want to emulate, to get closer to them.

Many Mansions, then, represents these various stages of evolvement. People talk about spheres, but I have always felt that the term spheres is a little misleading in that it gives a clear demarcation line. There are no such demarcations in spiritual life and consciousness because you are always just that little bit ahead of yourself, though not to the degree that causes undue effort beyond your capabilities.

You cannot get to a sphere or state of spiritual consciousness beyond your normal capacity; were you to do so you would disintegrate. The light or power would be too strong for you and you would be shattered.

You may say: "But surely, in this state there must be some objective? You can't just wander around. It sounds very dull and boring."

Again, we are dealing with something that is far beyond physical expression, but I assure you that there is a wholeness of existence that is absolutely impossible for you to understand now. Yet, apart from that, we are aware in this state of the needs (to use your expression) of the lower spheres. We are constantly awake to this demand.

This is part of our understanding of spiritual love. Spiritual love can only be effective if it is aware of the needs of those around; so there is this full and wonderful joy of participation. You have everyone near you with whom you are in tune. You have this dear and loving example of the next step, those who are so deeply attached to you just that step ahead, beckoning and encouraging you, although you are not yet able to interpret this in those terms. It gives you the same sense of joy as when you think about Spring and Summer; you know it is only a question of time before this is going to be reality. But there is no sense of painful longing, nothing distressing or disturbing, only an appreciation that "This is there for me. I know it is within my reach as soon as I am ready to apply myself to it".

Everything in the physical is a reflection of the spirit, but not in the form that you recognise it. Think about painting, music, poetry, literature - all the things that bring out the best from the people who create them. In this stage of Many Mansions you do not read books, look at paintings or hear music, but you know exactly what the artist was trying to express in spiritual terms with his painting, his music, and all the other gifts that go with it.

Compassion, sympathy, understanding, all are part of this appreciation that is generated in colour and beauty around you. We have trees and flowers, we have grass, but not like yours. It is something that is created out of the love and beauty, that through painting, music and literature we have clumsily tried to express - clumsily in terms of comparison with this beauty of artistic creative force around us here in spiritual terms.

The trees reflect colour, light and love. You are part of the tree, in tune with it; it feeds you. You respond to it in that you recognise it as a reflection of God's love as you are a reflection of God's love. It emits a sound like a beautiful tiny bell, again quite impossible to describe, but you hear it within yourself and respond spiritually.

The flowers can dance and sing in their own particular way

without any of the expressions of dancing and singing as you know them. But everything gives you of itself in a conscious overwhelming generosity of joy and you reciprocate, sharing everything around you with this giving and taking. There are fountains of spiritual replenishment, drops of water that change colour. You stand under them and are revitalised. The drops as they fall upon you give you a living force and happiness, and you are elated by this as you are all part of it.

These, then, are your mansions - mansions depending on the level of your own response and appreciation, each of them as beautiful for you as you are able to accept. You cannot accept more than you are able to understand and reciprocate, so that everything is dependent upon your spiritual progress.

I have explained before that there is this period that we know as Hell. Hell is a recognition of your imperfections and the pain that you experience from that recognition. But periodically, you have to have times when your strength is restored.

You are not able at this stage to reach out on your own behalf for spiritual strength, but in your desperation and desolation you cry, "Oh God, please help me!" or even, "Please forgive me. Show me how I might put it right!"

In this lovely Elysian state of spiritual perfection, the cry comes out to us like your telephone ringing or an S.O.S. going out from a ship. Then, those of us who are on that wavelength relative to your spiritual grouping immediately congregate and send out love and power. So persons wandering in the darkness and desolation of their particular Hell, perhaps find themselves sitting in a garden, not necessarily remembering who they are, but something of the pain or ache is taken out for a little while.

This is the result of the joy that has been poured from this source of spiritual attainment that Many Mansions represents. There are those whose specific work it is to accompany this power and be with these people if such is their need. But that is another story.

There are, too, times when we are told that one of our group is joining us; our dear friend who has been passing through the tribulation of redemption is coming home to us. This move from the state of Hell is rather like another form of death.

So, just as your physical death is a discarding of your body, so this spiritual discarding is a kind of wholeness that is equivalent to being born. You are born into this spiritual state of ecstasy and fulfilment. You are indeed coming to these Many Mansions that contain everything and everyone with whom you are in tune. It is very difficult for you on earth to understand because you think in terms of "Well, what do you do? How do you spend your time?".

Time for us is non-existent. We are aware of the needs of the whole universe to the level of our ability to feel these needs and appreciate them. Everything is dependent upon one's capacity. We know what we are doing, but it is not doing with our hands. Imagine rings of light.

Here we have the bright sunshine of this highest attainment, and there we have the bright sunshine of the next state of spiritual consciousness that we know as Heaven and Hell. Next, we have the Summerland where you are welcomed by all your friends. Then, you have the Astral where you have access to your dear ones on the earth plane, but where you are rather cut off from spiritual attainment. Yet another ring is the earthly existence. All rings of Light, darkening as they lower their rate of vibration.

Through all this is the Golden Cord of spiritual grouping. Coming back to Many Mansions, Jesus meant that each soul belongs to its own spiritual group which remains the same throughout eternity. You are spiritually grouped here upon the earth plane with certain people; sometimes you do not meet them but sometimes you do and you recognise them. There is no introduction, no getting to know one another for you have known them for a long time. These are they who are your spiritual family.

So, from the lowest to the highest is a Golden Cord that is responsive to your every need upon every level. You can go upwards and downwards. You are responsive in that group to everything that you or the rest of your group may need, whether they be on the earth plane or way ahead of you by evolvement.

You are always attached, and the electric shock of participation connects you, however highly evolved your spiritual companions may be. You are never separate from this pipe of power that is either coming to you or going from you.

Therefore, although you have shed physical memories, although you have passed through the chastening experience of perfecting so that you might enjoy what this physical life represents by way of spiritual evolvement, you are never separate from those people who are your people.

Some of you say to me, "I am so worried that my husband, my lover, my dear one will be so far advanced when I get there that they will have left me behind."

This is almost impossible because the range of physical living - you call it three score years and ten - is so infinitesimal in terms of the eternal progression to which I have been referring,, that the furthest your dear ones could go would be to the Summerland. Not many of them have reached the stage where they are aware of their imperfections and their true spiritual identity.

Most of you will wait for those you have left behind, accompanying them and sharing the experience together. This is always dependent on your spiritual grouping, and not affected by any physical relationship whatsoever.

Physical relationship in many cases is merely a physical means to an end, a means whereby you may best effect your spiritual purpose. Obviously, there will be some to whom you are spiritually related in the earth experience, and if this is so you are indeed fortunate because you will know something of this exquisite joy and harmony, however restricted by the physical experience it is.

Many Mansions, then, is a state of existence whereby you, the spirit, enjoy everything of which you are capable, participating in exquisite love and joy, where there can be no unkind thought or mean action. Everything is so rarefied that it is quite impossible for me to portray its perfection.

Hence Jesus' remark to his friends. "In My Father's house are many mansions, I go to prepare a place for you. I go to make myself ready to receive you, at that joyous occasion when you stand recognised in your own particular spiritual state of consciousness. When you stand recognised in your own divinity and know the perfect joy that comes from that participation."

However dark or lonely the path, however torn you may feel from the vicissitudes, difficulties and disappointments that go to make up the pattern of your life, remember that one day you are going to stand fulfilled. The only thing that is going to cause you pain is that you have not made full use of the opportunities that this life has afforded you.

Life means, therefore, going on, picking yourself up when you feel you cannot go another step. Trying again, when you feel that every ounce of your strength has been used up. It means, too, being constantly aware that however limited your understanding, you are never absent from that Golden Thread of Love containing everything that is perfect and best which you can draw to yourself when you find that life is too much for you.

So, think in terms of the fullest appreciation of this Fountain of Love that is ever yours for the asking. Try to envisage this state of spiritual ecstasy and perfection, and draw to yourself the strength that it represents.

I assure you, one day you will stand upon that threshold and say: "Yes, indeed, it was worthwhile. Everything I did was worth the effort, because this is joy so exquisite, so overwhelmingly beautiful that everything I paid for it was of little cost compared to what I have earned as a result of my efforts."

Some other titles published by
LIGHT PUBLISHING

INSIGHT AND INTUITION by Julie Soskin
Julie's eagerly-awaited manual on psychic and spiritual development is
virtually a do-it-yourself manual of cosmic consciousness. Exercises in
each chapter help us internalise the essence of what we have read and
integrate it into our daily lives.
£9.99 paperback, ISBN 0 903336 14 6

IN TOUCH WITH RAYNOR C. JOHNSON by Sheila Gwillam
With a Foreword by Paul Beard. Wisdom and spiritual insight from a
renowned scientist, author and spiritual philosopher.
£8.99 paperback, ISBN 0 903336 15 4

IZARIS by Keith Casburn
Communications from Izar, one of the second magnitude stars in our
universe, tell us how we relate vibrationally to stars and galaxies, and
the demands this makes on us mentally, emotionally and physically.
£8.99 paperback, ISBN 0 903336 12 X

MEDIUMSHIP MADE SIMPLE by Ivy Northage
Widely regarded as one of the classic texts on practical mediumship.
Ivy Northage draws on 40 years as medium and teacher, giving clear
descriptions of psychic development and its practical applications.
£7.99 paperback, ISBN 0 903336 19 7

THE NEW SCIENCE OF THE SPIRIT by David A. Ashe
An exciting new approach providing a framework for the universe in
which the laws of physics and the laws of spirit become one.
£9.95 hardback, ISBN 0 903336 56 1
£6.99 paperback, ISBN 0 903336 55 3

PRINCIPLES OF THE UNIVERSE by Keith Casburn
Communications from a source beyond the time-frame of our solar
system: the multidimensional nature of being; how to become the
spiritual beings we really are.
£6.99 paperback, ISBN 0 903336 28 6

SOUL TREK by Julie Gale
A channelled book tracing the soul's evolution from the Source, through physical incarnation and beyond. New light is shed on subjects such as Group Souls, Twin Souls, and Reincarnation.
£8.99 paperback, ISBN 0 903336 26 X

SOULWORK: FOUNDATIONS FOR SPIRITUAL GROWTH by Sue Minns
166 page tabulated Workbook and six audiocassettes based on the Foundation Course run by Sue Minns at the College of Psychic Studies. Step-by-step guidance and direction for your own experience of the recollection of the soul: Breathing, Meditation, The Aura, Chakras, Healing, Psychic Energy, Body/Mind, Inner Child and Soul, Karma & Reincarnation.
£39.99 paperback & six audiocassettes, ISBN 0 903336 16

SPIRITUAL REALISATION: INNER VALUES IN EVERYDAY LIFE
Communications by CHAN, spirit guide of Ivy Northage
CHAN's suggestions for handling life's problems carry spiritual authority but are never over-assertive. A book to treasure.
£7.50 paperback, ISBN 0 903336 21 9

TRANSFORMATION by Julie Soskin
The fourth channelled work by Julie Soskin reveals the enormous shift now occurring in the evolution of humanity, and the changes this will bring in our lives.
£6.99 paperback, ISBN 0 903336 24 3

The College of Psychic Studies
16 Queensberry Place, South Kensington, London SW7 2EB
Telephone: 0171-589 3292/3; Fax: 0171-589 2824